Haiku Poetry for the
Covid Pandemic

Haiku Poetry for the Covid Pandemic

WITNESSING AND CONNECTING

Kate Dash

Haiku Poetry for the Covid Pandemic

Copyright 2022 by Kate Dash

All rights reserved

No part of this book may be used, scanned, uploaded, reproduced, or distributed in any manner whatsoever without written permission from the author or publisher except in brief quotations embodied in critical analyses or reviews.

FIRST EDITION, 2022

Printed in the United States of America

Publisher: Word Haven Media

Book Design: Nicole Hayward

Author photo by Zee

Library of Congress Cataloging-in-Publication Data available upon request

ISBN: 978-1-7325714-8-8 (epub)
ISBN: 978-1-7325714-9-5 (paperback)

Dedicated to
pandemic healthcare workers
around the world

The way through the world
is more difficult to find
than the way beyond it.
—Wallace Stevens

But what does it mean, the plague?
It's life, that's all.
—Albert Camus

There are some things you learn best in calm,
and some in storm.
—Willa Cather

CONTENTS

Preface | xiii

COVID BEGINS—MARCH 2020 | 1

World Switching Off | 3
Barricades | 3
Curtain Drop | 3
No Stores in Stores | 4

DINING IN THE TIME OF COVID | 5
Serious Reservations | 5
Table Blunders | 5
At Home | 5
Disinfecting the Groceries | 5
Home-cooked | 6
Favorite Restaurant Reopening | 6

LOVE IN THE TIME OF COVID | 8
Epigraph, by Rumi | 8
Riffing on Rumi—Resurrection Time | 8
Expiration Date | 11
Please Be My Covid Danger Zone! | 12
Finally, We Meet | 13

TIME IN THE TIME OF COVID | 14
Paradoxical | 14
Blurred | 14
Flat | 14
Staggered | 14
Artless | 15

DRESSING FOR COVID | 16
Masking Advice | 16
Covid Wear | 16
Masked Conversation | 16
Another Earring Lost | 17
Castoff Mask | 17

SOCIAL NORMS | 18
Distancing | 18
Paranoia | 18
Longing | 18
Traveling Nowhere | 19
Schooled by the Virus | 19

WORKING FROM HOME | 20
Impossible | 20
Daylong Zoom-Ba | 20
Somewhere a Cat | 21
WFH Attire | 22
Resignation | 22

PUBLIC HEALTH | 23
Expertise | 23
Terrible Advice | 23
Crisis Mode | 23
Vaccines | 24
Data Overkill | 24
Official Guidance | 24
Homeless Survey | 25
Distortion | 25
Connected | 25

NURSING HOMES | 26
Visitation Policy | 26
Dying Alone | 27

HOSPITALS | 28
The Soundtrack | 28
Unquiet Deaths | 28
In/different Hands | 28
Fulminant Covid | 29
Impromptu Morgues | 29
Medically Speaking | 29
Health Providers | 30
Heroes at First | 31

2020 SEASONS OF DISCONTENT | 33
Spring | 33
Summer | 33
Fall | 33
Winter | 33
End of year? | 34

MIDDLE COVID—2021 | 35

A SECOND BLURRED YEAR
STILL, THINGS ACTUALLY HAPPENED | 37
Wake-up Call | 37
January | 37
February | 37
March | 38
April | 38
May | 38
June | 39
July | 40
August | 41
September | 41
October | 41
November | 42
December | 42

STILL MUDDLING THROUGH COVID | 43
   Adrift | 43
   Nostalgic | 44
   Irritated | 44
   Alienated | 44
   Afraid | 44
   In Grief | 45
   Panicked | 45
   Exhausted | 45
   Shaken | 45
   Numb | 46
   Hopeless | 46
   Joyless | 46
   Stunned | 46
   Whiplashed | 47
   Pandemic Playlist | 47

ADVICE ABOUT COVID | 48
   Trying to View Covid as an Opportunity to . . . | 48
   Or to . . . | 48

COVID—2022 | 49

   January—Another "New" Year? | 51
   Disunited States of America | 51
   February—War in Europe? | 52
   Unrelenting Covid | 52
   Death Tolls | 53
   Cavernous Inequality | 53
   March—Suspended Animation | 54

COVID 3.0—MARCH 2022 | 55

Acknowledgments | 60

PREFACE

ON WEDNESDAY, MARCH 11, 2020, I was dining with friends on a docked cruise ship, courtesy of a charity auction win. The festive mood was regularly punctured by troubling news about Covid-19 that continued to pop up on our cellphones. That day, the National Basketball Association suspended its current season. The stock market plunged. The World Health Organization proclaimed that the coronavirus "outbreak" had reached "pandemic" proportions.

Our table of ten on the Commodore Cabernet Sauvignon was one of many dozens. In the ship's packed dining room, roving waiters generously poured wine, and plentiful food was provided buffet-style on common serving tables. We couldn't have predicted that this event would come to signify our last day of "normal" in pre-Covid time. Within 24 hours, "the novel coronavirus" shook the globe, upending our lives. Large gatherings of friends and family, indoor dining, public crowds, shared buffet tables, mask-less servers and patrons—became unthinkable for most people and public health experts.

Having had to schedule our dinner weeks in advance, we also had no inkling that we'd be docked a stone's throw away from a sea-faring cruise ship carrying hundreds of coronavirus-infected passengers and crew. Just a few days before our event, news broke about the Grand Princess circling in a holding pattern near the Golden Gate Bridge, waiting for permission to dock somewhere, anywhere. On board and literally "at sea" were 3,500-plus passengers and a boatload of the new coronavirus. After San Francisco denied the ship's request to dock, on March 9 the Grand Princess was headed for the Port of Oakland. The official (but overly-optimistic) plan was to offboard all passengers within three days, meaning that hundreds of distressed and ill people would be actively disembarking for transport to hospitals or quarantine centers at the time of our dinner gathering. In such close proximity, we wondered whether attending our dinner was reckless or insensitive—or perhaps both.

Though some of us suspected that fast-moving storm clouds were heading our way, life in the U.S. still proceeded rather routinely on the date of the Grand Princess' arrival. On March 10, the eve of our dinner, only three residents in our entire county—encompassing Oakland and Berkeley—had tested positive for the virus. Elsewhere, a suburb north of New York City was just emerging as a small "cluster" of Covid cases, ostensibly at a "safe distance" from the City. Italy's number of infections exceeded 10,000—more than anywhere except China where the outbreak was first recognized. We could still imagine and hope that "the novel coronavirus" might be contained.

But as we soon discovered, the virus ambushed us all. It unmoored us and sent us sailing into uncertain waters, without rudder or direction. During the subsequent two years, it tested us—personally, physically, mentally, financially, politically, existentially. Many of us couldn't or didn't survive the challenges, but each of us was somehow affected. The current spinning world of March 2022 is markedly different than the one that was spinning two years ago. We've entered new history that continues to reveal itself with painstaking immediacy.

I wrote these haiku poems as exercises over the two years since our dinner on the cruise ship, trying to put into words my experience of Covid that often felt wordless or unfathomable. The poems are admittedly rough and tumble, and sometimes inelegant—written to support my psychic survival, without aim for poetry contests or anthologies. Through a practice of trying to stay present in unique moments during the annihilating fog of those years, I also wrote them in witness.

I hope readers will find some resonant lines to hold onto, if only to feel more connected to the universal experience of Covid through which we are all muddling.

—KATE DASH, MARCH 2022

COVID BEGINS—MARCH 2020

World Switching Off

People succumbing
fast to Covid in China.
A fearful world watches,

prays for containment.
Shock! The virus escapes!
With alarming speed

it travels to Europe.
Ten northern Italian towns
shut off from the world.

Barricades

Close windows and doors!
Barricade against air, light.
Stagnate in cages.

Look, through the keyhole:
another country is closing.
Global pandemic.

Curtain Drop

Curtain drops from the sky.
Schools, diners, theaters close.
Pandemic showtime.

No Stores in Stores

The store shelves empty.
People hoarding everything.
Toilet paper: Gone!

DINING IN THE TIME OF COVID

Serious Reservations

Pandemic parklets.
Dining in rain, wind, and snow.
Starving for contact.

Table Blunders

We ordered cosmos
but forgot to remove masks.
Cranberry-stained scarves.

At Home

We learn to bake bread.
It satisfies for a while.
What we crave is cake.

Disinfecting the Groceries

Bleach on the apples.
Wiping-down the milk and eggs.
Ritual cleansings

of dubious worth.
(Though no reports of groceries
succumbing to Covid.)

Home-cooked

Sipping grief and loss
we thirst for a respite.
Pop! Bottle uncorks!

Home dinners with wine
become "a thing" every night
helping us to cope.

Every next morning
we agree to cut back
—after just one more night.

Favorite Restaurant Reopening

The waiters wear masks.
The daily special now: Fear.
Gloved hands serve salad.

Tables far apart.
Sanitizer-scented soup.
Ugh! Wish I'd stayed home.

7   Covid Begins — March 2020

LOVE IN THE TIME OF COVID

The way of love is not
a subtle argument.

The door there
is devastation.

Birds make great sky-circles
of their freedom.
How do they learn it?

They fall, and falling,
they're given wings.

—*Rumi*

Riffing on Rumi—Resurrection Time

"Subtle" would be good.
Instead, my resentment brews
inside our cramped home.

Before the lockdown,
when I could steal time away—
from you, from this house—

I could endure us,
tame my dreary unhappiness,
and keep everything in place.

But now, no escape.
Living with you is slow death.
I can't stay, can't leave.

Looking desperately
to "the door there" I shudder—
devastation so close!

But as the moments pass,
devastation reshapes
and begins to look like freedom.

Thunderclap truth!
For far too long I've been falling,
trying to stay in place.

Now, through the window,
I see birds circling the sky.
I long to join them.

Mistake! All the time
I've been praying for saving wings
to help me escape,

not realizing
this precondition for flight:
Our devastation.

Resurrection time!
I fling open the door there.
Self-destruct, take flight!

Expiration Date

We had just one date
before Covid intervened,
March twenty-twenty.

But, my god, I swooned!
You intoxicated me
over drinks that night!

Everything in me
that could feel, felt something new.
How I desired you!

Then the next morning:
Crack! The world began to break.
Covid at our door.

The brisk quarantine.
The lockdown, isolation.
The dizzying news.

Denial, at first.
Nothing could keep us apart.
Our passion, that strong.

But the strange weeks passed
and the virus persisted,
separating us.

Our FaceTime dates? Meh.
Thrill transitioned to dread.
"We" felt remote, surreal.

Seeing you on screen,
flattened in two dimensions,
I came to view you

like a character
in an old rom-com movie
already fading.

I too often felt
crazy, actually doubting
my memory of you.

Still, my heart recalls
its first time cradling
sorrow-mingled joy.

Please Be My Covid Danger Zone!

Be my danger zone!
Come close, touch me, breathe on me.
Save me with your tongue.

Finally, We Meet

The first time we met
after five long lonely months,
smiles hid behind masks.

Brr! Freezing outdoors!
Hugging through down, flannel, wool
arms couldn't enclose you.

TIME IN THE TIME OF COVID

Paradoxical

Feeling endlessness.
Yet, too, the end of the days.
Paradoxical time.

Blurred

Our days in limbo
their discrete edges erased
merging into one.

Flat

Weight of constant waiting
flattens time under lockdown.
Hours lose dimension.

Staggered

Time skids, stumbles through
these unchartered ways to live.
Unsteady time.

Artless

Remembering when
in twenty-nineteen that we
used to meet for lunch.

On a whim, we'd ride
a crowded subway train and
head to a museum.

And how we huddled
around art that we loved.
Pre-pandemic time.

DRESSING FOR COVID

Masking Advice

Mask on, off, on, off.
Then on again? (Hard to tell.)
Unmasked confusion.

Covid Wear

Sweatpants and tee-shirt,
daily Covid uniform.
Dressed not-to-impress.

Masked Conversation

Every time we meet
on the patio, masks on
and six feet apart,

loud construction noise
sounds in the background
and planes fly overhead.

Sigh. I do not hear
more than half of what you say.
Still, our friendship speaks.

Another Earring Lost

Six earrings now lost
to straps on masks, hats, glasses
tangled under chin.

Castoff Mask

Blue mask on sidewalk.
Life-saving mission fulfilled.
Now worn and castoff.

SOCIAL NORMS

Distancing

Social distancing
standing at six feet apart
feels like six "under"—

social deadening.
A death toll not reflected
by any official stats.

Paranoia

Locked down. Quarantined.
A trip to the store could kill!
Paranoia lurks.

Longing

Longing to receive
bottles bearing messages
from someone, somewhere.

I need to be reached.
To be surprised by contact
unscripted and human.

Traveling Nowhere

Beyond our locked doors
the vastness of the globe shrinks.
No travel allowed.

Schooled by the Virus

Virtual learning,
internet connections—
Poof! The classroom disappears.

Schools close, open, close.
Exasperated parents
and students suffer.

Masked children worry
whether it's safe to return
while the PTA brawls.

Pandemic schooling:
Time circles back and repeats.
Schools reopen, reclose.

WORKING FROM HOME

Impossible

WFH? That's crazy!
With three children and a dog,
only work to stay sane.

Daylong Zoom-Ba

The constant Zoom meets.
Colleagues in tiny boxes
like checkerboard tiles.

Everyone smiling
and seeming to stare at me
all at once—too much!

Trish needs a haircut.
Bob *still* can't unmute himself?!
Christopher's gained weight.

On camera, too,
I smile and nod, look alert,
hoping the wi-fi fails.

I am on all day
performing my one-woman show,
no intermission.

Yikes! What's our topic now?
The meeting agenda zooms in, out,
making me dizzy.

Somewhere a Cat

While the boss critiques
my work during a videocall,
I hear loud purring.

Distracted, I search the screen
for evidence of a cat
somewhere in the background.

Purring grows louder
while the boss drones on and on . . .
Still, no cat on screen.

Unable to picture
my sour boss with sweet kitty:
Cognitive failure.

Snap to attention!
The boss suddenly frowns and says,
"Sorry to tell you this."

But what did she say?
And where the hell is that cat?
No one purring now.

WFH Attire

Zoom-ready to meet:
same daytime pajama bottoms,
clean shirt for camera.

Resignation

My job, a treadmill.
I trudge nowhere, furiously.
Ah! Great resignation!

PUBLIC HEALTH

Expertise

Only Covid knows
what Covid's going to do.
No human experts.

Terrible Advice

It will just go away.
If not, try bleach, perhaps light.
No need to worry!

Crisis Mode

So, this is what a
"public health crisis" looks like:
No common wisdom

guiding the commons,
and failure to recognize
clear dangers in view.

Vaccines

Pfizer. Moderna.
Vocabulary of hope
some choose to reject.

Then breakthrough infections,
immunity on the wane,
booster protections.

Still, everyone searches
for another immunity—
to sorrow and loss.

Data Overkill

Overwhelmed by an
avalanche of statistics!
Numbing data points

point to nowhere, really.
Nothing adds up anymore.
Time only subtracts.

Official Guidance

CDC advice—
its rules and risks change daily.
Confusion does not.

Homeless Survey

Homeless before, homeless still.
No different with the pandemic.
Same needs, same hunger.

Distortion

Art of distortion
on display in the public square.
Facts twisted and blurred.

People wander through
partisan post-truth nation,
deciding what to view.

Connected

We are connected.
The myth of isolation
counters reality.

A distant stranger's cough
quickly spreads across the globe
spraying lethal proof.

NURSING HOMES

Visitation Policy

Within nursing homes,
forgotten existences.
Residents at risk.

No visitors allowed.
Death, the exception, of course—
and no stranger here.

Haunting images.
Abandoned people languish,
suspended in despair.

Dying Alone

She draws her last breath
staring through a closed window
while we stand outside.

Her isolation
something more than suffering . . .
Grief, defying words.

Separated from
everything she loves,
her final lament unheard.

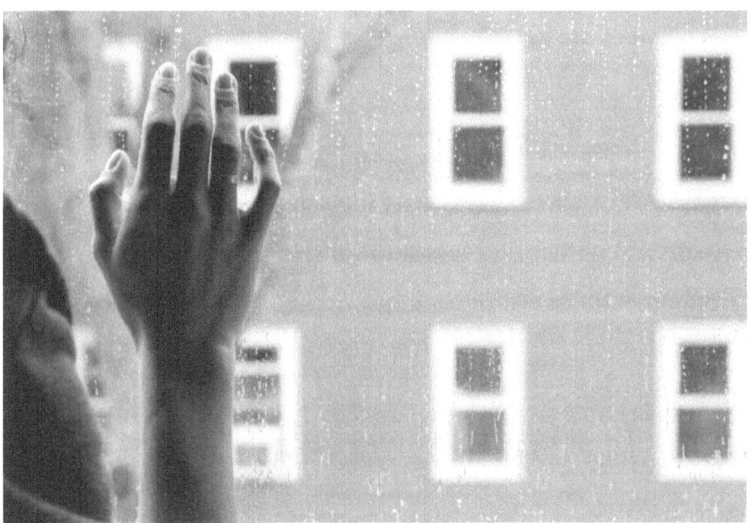

HOSPITALS

The Soundtrack

ICU soundtrack:
Cough, wheeze, moan, beeping machines,
shuddering last gasps.

Unquiet Deaths

Loved ones die alone.
Their cold, silent bodies speak
the catastrophe.

In/different Hands

They won't let me near.
I watch him on an iPhone
leaving, forever.

The hands holding his
are not mine when he finally lets go.
Unthinkable, still.

The last thing he feels:
the touch of Purell-soaked hands.
Sterile comfort.

Fulminant Covid

She wakes up coughing.
Noon, her appetite disappears.
Night, we sing vespers.

Impromptu Morgues

We pitch canvas tents
in hospital parking lots
to store the dead bodies.

Refrigerated trucks
transport the cadavers
wherever they can.

Packed mortuaries,
overwhelmed with casualties,
are forced to close doors.

Medically Speaking

Lingering illness
after infection resolves:
"Post-COVID syndrome."

Fatigued. Fuzzy brain.
Chest pain. Cough. Troubled breathing.
"Covid long-hauler."

Health Providers

Patients crowd hallways,
praying for ventilators,
oxygen and life.

They push call buttons
that will remain unanswered—
too many staff out sick.

Doctors scurry, fret,
juggling life-and-death choices.
Still, clocks dictate time.

Which patients to save?
Who among them deserves
the ventilator?

Shell-shocked nurses watch
the bloodless executions
continue to mount.

Overwhelmed, sleepless,
traumatized—the staff burn out,
sicken or take leave.

Bottomless sadness.
Impossible demands exceed
capacity to care.

Spent of compassion,
the heart takes armor, retreats.
Only dry tears now.

Heroes at First

They praised us at first.
From rooftops, they clapped and proclaimed
"You are our heroes!"

Every night at six
they shouted, banged pots, blared horns
in great gratitude.

Then the ritual stopped.
Suddenly they viewed us as
suspects in a war—

a pandemic war
that held everyone hostage
to misinformation

conspiracies
and brute alienation
from one another.

We were heroes once,
even sacrificial lambs,
when terror prevailed.

Does anyone ask
who will change the bandages
after we are gone?

2020 SEASONS OF DISCONTENT

Spring

Long, lonely lockdown.
Empty baseball stadiums.
Trees blossom outside.

Summer

Surely this pandemic will pass?
Please stop this nightmare gone viral!
Covid's heels dig in.

Fall

More bedeviled plans.
Another plane flight canceled.
Going nowhere fast.

Winter

Why is the virus STILL here?
Noxious, infuriating pest!
Shoo! Get out of our lives!

End of year?

Twenty-twenty ends.
Virus ignores calendar
and slips into next year.

MIDDLE COVID—2021

A SECOND BLURRED YEAR
STILL, THINGS ACTUALLY HAPPENED

Wake-up Call

Time to clear the fog
and awaken to the hours!
Twenty-twenty-one.

January

An insurrection.
Mob storms U.S. Capitol.
Democracy shakes.

February

For rousing the mob,
a second Trump impeachment.
Slap! Wrist briefly stings.

~~~~~

Texas in deep freeze.
Buccaneers win Super Bowl.
World flips upside down.

March

Coronavirus'
one-year anniversary
of shutdowns. NO CHEERS.

~ ~ ~ ~ ~

A container ship
wedges in the Suez Canal.
Snap! Supply chain breaks.

April

In Covid's swift wake
three million people are dead.
Children, parents, friends . . .

Families left stunned.
Lovers grieve vacated beds.
Measureless anguish.

May

Remembering George Floyd,
killed on Memorial Day,
May twenty-twenty.

Breathing deeply for
nine minutes, twenty-nine seconds—
memorializing his death.

~ ~ ~ ~ ~

Addiction, anguish,
and soaring suicide rates
sounding deep despair.

Record overdose deaths:
100,000 last year.
Atmospheric grief.

June

Gunfire everywhere.
Bullet holes riddle the map.
Cincinnati. Austin. Alabama. Colorado. Baton Rouge. Anchorage . . .

~ ~ ~ ~ ~

On a Miami shore,
a condo building collapses.
Aging structure fails.

Stunned residents
fall, flee, and fear for their lives,
if lucky to survive.

~ ~ ~ ~ ~

Delta variant
in U.S. accounts for ten
percent of cases.

CDC christens it
a "variant of concern."
(Prescient prediction.)

600,000
Americans already dead.
Virus surges again.

July

"Summer of Freedom"
doesn't arrive in the U.S.
Vaccines sit on shelves.

~ ~ ~ ~ ~

The CDC reports
a life expectancy drop,
the largest since WWII.

Lifelines, vanishing.
Losing time to live and love.
Optimism frays.

The present now looks to
a future containing loss
birthed in our Covid past.

August

Metaverse arrives
to *augment* reality?
Please! Not *more* of that!

~ ~ ~ ~ ~

Twenty years of war
in Afghanistan ends. Cut!
The stunned nation bleeds.

September

Major Covid peak.
Delta variant explodes!
More bruised suns.

October

The nation's death toll mounts.
Seven-hundred thousand dead.
Some people look away;

others search the sky
for the new planet, dreaming
worlds without Covid.

November

A trillion-dollar
infrastructure bill passes.
Can it prop us up?

~ ~ ~ ~ ~

Inflation inflates
reaching a forty-year high.
Has the worst happened yet?

No. Omicron, now.
A new "variant of
concern" concerns us.

December

Concern yields to fear.
Omicron virus ascends!
Holiday lights dim.

Parties canceled for
Christmas, Channukah, Kwanza.
Only Gloom gathers.

U.S. death toll now
exceeds eight-hundred thousand—
the world's highest toll.

Under the continued siege
we feel the return of dread.
More days in crisis.

STILL MUDDLING THROUGH COVID

Adrift

Illness, death, grief, loss
darkening our spirits.
No lighthouse in sight.

Months of dodging touch
rearranging the deck chairs
fearing each other's breath.

Adrift on rough seas
passengers in disaster
we seek any port.

Nostalgic

Do you remember
talking together for hours,
never mentioning Covid?

Irritated

My fuse short, last nerve frayed,
I'm too stressed to meditate.
Warning! Back away!

Alienated

Isolated in
cold lonely dark places,
and becoming alien

as people detach
and hibernate in bubbles
opaque and apart.

Afraid

Please tell me your cough
is a cold or allergy!
Don't worry me sick!

In Grief

Trying to tame the
emotional bloodletting
and integrate loss.

Panicked

Panic and chaos.
Life suspended, upended.
World out of control.

Exhausted

The complexity
of daily tasks quadruples.
Pandemic fatigue.

Shaken

Rules. Statistics.
Warnings. Opinions. Advice.
Openings. Closings.

Nothing is stable.
Trauma of everyday life
lived in upheaval.

Numb

Not feeling sometimes
to defend against overwhelm.
Then deep breathe, re-feel.

Hopeless

They say silver lines
every cloud in the sky.
Alas! Cloudless skies.

Joyless

In a self-willed trance
watching the days drain of color.
Joyless aimlessness.

Stunned

Shops and diners closed.
No weddings, church, funerals.
Eerie nothingness.

Whiplashed

"Breakthrough" infections now?
Will we ever tame the virus?
Whiplash! Spikes, troughs, spikes!

Pandemic Playlist

Silence. Then dirges.
Resurrection music follows.
Click! Playlist repeats.

ADVICE ABOUT COVID

Trying to View Covid as an Opportunity to . . .

Embrace solitude
confront loss and finitude.
(Would rather eat sweets.)

Or to . . .

Reassess one's life,
while braving these deep, dark woods—
true way, wholly lost

keeping Dante in mind,
struggling toward purpose and light,
Divine Comedy.

COVID—2022

January—Another "New" Year?

Delta. Omicron.
Another Covid winter.
Virus everywhere!

And now two years in—
still a thousand deaths each day
in the U.S. alone.

Has anything changed?
No ritual for this day.
New year, same old distress.

Disunited States of America

Vaccines plentiful
while just sixty-two percent
of Americans

vaccinate fully.
Knife-deep hostilities brew,
the nation divides.

Cumulative rage,
obsessive speculation,
new realms of grievance,

the absurd war begins
between the vaxxed and unvaxxed.
Disunity reigns.

Casualties of the war:
resilience and compassion,
genuine discourse.

February—War in Europe?

Bombs dropping in Europe?
Russia invading Ukraine?
Unfathomable!

But you see the proof:
cities destroyed, homes aflame.
Ukrainians bleeding.

Brutal foolishness.
Extravagant violence.
Inhumanity.

Unrelenting Covid

Now six million deaths
worldwide (an undercount).
Pandemic still strong.

Children who have lost
a parent or caregiver
to Covid-19

numbering more than
five million across the globe.
Loss, bewildering.

Death Tolls

U.S. death toll mounts
skirting one million casualties
from Covid-19—

the same proportion
of the population dead
as from World War II.

Cavernous Inequality

Owned in the U.S. by
top one-percent of earners:
one third of all wealth.

Meanwhile, every night
more than 100,000
children are homeless.

How to explain this
thudding inequality
to the shivering child?

March—Suspended Animation

Our lives in storage.

Not exactly "surviving."

Impatient to live.

COVID 3.0—MARCH 2022

Tenacious virus!
Covid 3.0 begins.
My resilience wanes.

How many surges,
how many more variants
in the year/s ahead?

Which countries will close,
collapse or disappear?
Who will get to live?

How many boosters
will I need, how many masks?
How will I survive?

Tired of the questions
that keep repeating.
Uncertainty rules.

Tired of the virus
trespassing my psyche
in bloodied combat boots.

I have poured the wine.
I have lit the votive candles.
I've sacrificed to B-list gods.

I've been vaxxed
and boosted.

I've struggled to be patient,
weathering the disaster,
letting go of time
for TWO YEARS.

But
now.

Too many clocks, and not enough time.

Too many sacrifices, and not enough faith.

So
now.

A choice.

To enter Covid 3.0
with the same armor and fear

or to open "the door there"
and dance
with the devil who refuses to leave.

And
now
I know the risks on both sides of that door.
I understand that safety is an illusion.
People can wither or die in their fortified homes.
Buildings can collapse.

A person can fall ill while stranded at sea.
You can awaken to an army in your backyard.

Pondering that door now,
I begin to remember joy.

I remember
"great sky-circles"
and flight.

Pondering that door,
I feel my heart stirring, shaking off its dust.

I shed my armor.

I wash my hands in the dust of the last two years and unlatch the door.

ACKNOWLEDGMENTS

I'm grateful to friends and family who sustained me through the pandemic, in commiseration and laughter. Thanks also to the healthcare workers who braved the brutal medical challenges of Covid-19.

My great appreciation to Diane Buczek and Leslie Larson for their helpful advice, and to Nicole Hayward who artfully designed this book.

Thankful acknowledgment is made to the artists whose photographs provided source material for the visuals in this book: Ali Karimiboroujeni, Sergi Brylev, Michael Held, Jonathan Farber, Sander Mathlene, Saneej Kallingal, Maksym Kaharlyt, and Mark Timberlake. To view their photographs in their unaltered original states, please visit https://unsplash.com

www.ingramcontent.com/pod-product-compliance
Lightning Source LLC
Chambersburg PA
CBHW020547080526
44583CB00013B/1037